This book belongs to:

_____

It was given to me by:

_____

On:

_____

Bible
Blessings
for Bedtime

LINDA CARLBLOM

ILLUSTRATED BY DAVID MILES

Bible
Blessings
for Bedtime

BARBOUR
PUBLISHING

Bless

"To give honor, glory, or favor." God blesses us by giving us His goodness. Jesus said that God blesses those who depend on Him, those who are sad, those who are gentle, and those who obey. People who are kind and have pure hearts are blessed. Peacemakers are blessed, too. So are people who are disapproved of for doing what is right. (Check out Matthew 5:1–10.) As Christians, we should ask God to bless anyone who mistreats us. Jesus blessed kids. And we can bless God by praising His goodness, and others by being kind to them.

from *Kids' Bible Dictionary*

Contents

"You're Welcome!"

"Anyone who welcomes a little child
like this in my name welcomes me."
Matthew 18:5 NIrV

Do you know that children are some of Jesus' favorite people? He loves them so much He told grown-ups they need to become like them if they want to get into the kingdom of heaven!

One day, Jesus' helpers asked Him, "Who is the most important person in the kingdom of heaven?" (Matthew 18:1 NIrv) Jesus called a little child to come and stand by Him. He probably knelt down, put His arm around the child, and snuggled him close. He told His helpers to listen up because what He was about to tell them was the truth. He said, "You need to change and become like little children. If you don't, you will never enter the kingdom of heaven. Anyone who becomes as free of pride as this child is the most important in the kingdom of heaven" (Matthew 18:3–4 NIrv).

Then He added with a smile, "Anyone who welcomes a little child like this in my name welcomes me" (Matthew 18:5 NIrv).

To welcome someone means you're glad they came. Children were important to Jesus in Bible times. And you're important to Him today! He'll welcome you into His arms and His kingdom when you let Him be in charge of your life.

God, I want to be in Your kingdom. Help me to let You be in charge of my life. I love You.

Moving Day

"I will make you a great nation, and I will bless you. I will make you famous. And you will be a blessing to others."

Genesis 12:2 ICB

Have you ever moved to a new place? In the Bible book of Genesis, God told Abraham to move away from all his friends. But He didn't tell Abraham where to go. He just said He would show him. Because God knew it would be hard for Abraham to leave his home, He gave him a special blessing to cheer him up. God said, "I will make you a great nation, and I will bless you. I will make you famous. And you will be a blessing to others."

Abraham didn't have to make that big move to a new place all alone. God went with him to help him. He even made Abraham a blessing to the new people he met. Abraham knew that God's plan for his life was good. He trusted God to do what was best for him. And God did!

Wherever you go, God goes with you. He always has a good plan for your life. He'll help you make new friends and be a special blessing to them. God is your forever friend no matter where you go.

God, being in a new place
can be scary. Help me to trust
You and the good plan You have
for me. Thanks for being my
forever friend.

Blessed by Accident

"May God give you plenty of rain
and good soil. Then you will
have plenty of grain and wine."
Genesis 27:28 ICB

Isaac had twin sons, Jacob and Esau. Even though they were twins, Esau was born a few minutes before Jacob, so he was the oldest, and the oldest son was supposed to get the father's blessing. But their mother, Rebekah, wanted their father to bless Jacob instead of Esau, so she came up with a plan.

Isaac was old and almost blind. Rebekah told Jacob to cook Isaac's favorite food and dress up like Esau to trick Isaac. Then Isaac would think Jacob was Esau and would bless him.

Their plan worked. Isaac smelled Esau's clothes on Jacob and thought it was his oldest son. Isaac knew God was the only One who could always provide everything we need, so he blessed Jacob, saying, "May God give you plenty of rain and good soil. Then you will have plenty of grain and wine."

It's not right to trick people as Jacob did. Before God could bless him, Jacob had to move far from home. He lived in fear of Esau's anger. But later Jacob humbled himself before God. He tried to make things right with Esau. Then God could give Jacob his father's blessing. Just as God gave rain, good soil, and food to Jacob, God will provide for your needs, too. What do you need today?

God, sometimes I do things I shouldn't. Thanks for promising that You'll take care of me even when I make mistakes. I love You.

Rubbed-Off Blessing

Then the Lord blessed the people in
Potiphar's house because of Joseph.

Genesis 39:5 ICB

Have you ever had something rub off on you? Maybe when you ate a chocolate bar your face or fingers ended up all chocolaty. Or maybe the picture you drew with a marker was still wet when you put your hand on it. Then you saw that you had the marker color on your hand!

A man named Potiphar put Joseph in charge of everything he owned. Joseph loved God and lived to serve Him. He worked hard and did his best at taking care of Potiphar's things. This made God happy, so He caused Joseph to do well at everything he did.

But then a funny thing happened. God's blessing on Joseph started rubbing off on Potiphar and his whole family.

Everything Potiphar did went well because of the good work Joseph did. Joseph's blessing became Potiphar's blessing, too!

Has one of your friends ever had good things happen because of you? If you love God, you will try to please Him by the way you live. Then His blessing may rub off of you and onto your friends! Wouldn't that be a nice gift to give a friend?

I love You, God, and want Your
blessing. Please bless my friends
because of my faith in You,
just as You did with Joseph
and Potiphar.

Brothers' Blessings

"Judah, your brothers will praise you.
You will grab your enemies by the neck.
Your brothers will bow down to you."

Genesis 49:8 ICB

Jacob had twelve sons. That's a big family! When he was old and about to die, Jacob asked all his sons to gather around him. He wanted to tell them what would happen to them in the future. For some of his sons, it was bad news. For others, like Judah, it was good.

"Judah." Jacob's voice was probably low as he lifted a weak hand and motioned for his son to come closer. "Your brothers will praise you. You will grab your enemies by the neck. Your brothers will bow down to you." He also said that Judah was brave like a lion and would be a great leader. Entire nations would obey him. Judah and his sons would always be king until the real King, Jesus, came to earth.

How would you feel if your brothers or sisters praised you, saying wonderful things about you, as Jacob said Judah's brothers would? Maybe they already do! It's good to get along with brothers and sisters, but it's not always easy. And it's even harder to get along with your enemies, people you don't like. Ask God to help you behave in a way that earns their praise!

Lord, sometimes I fight with my brothers and sisters. Help me to get along with them when we play. And show me how to be nice to my enemies.

"It's Not Fair!"

"Dan will do what is fair for his people."

Genesis 49:16 NIrV

In our Bibles, we learn Dan was one of twelve boys. When his father, Jacob, grew old and was ready to die, he gave blessings to his sons. He called them to his bedside one by one so they could receive their blessings. He started with Reuben, the oldest, and went clear down to the youngest, Benjamin. Dan was the seventh brother. I bet he could hardly wait his turn! What would his father say about his future?

"Dan," Jacob began, "you will do what is fair for your people." Dan may have smiled. His father trusted him! Jacob knew his son was honest and treated people fairly. That must have made Dan feel proud.

Are you fair to people? Do you take

turns? Are you a good sport or do you cry, "It's not fair!" when you don't win? Do you do what you say you'll do? If you can answer yes to all these questions, good for you! But if you had to say no to some, don't worry. God will help you become the boy or girl He wants you to be if you ask for His help.

God, I want to be someone
people trust, but I can't do it
by myself. Will You please
help me to be honest and fair?
Thanks!

Growing a Seed

"Asher's land will grow much good food.
He will grow food fit for a king."
Genesis 49:20 ICB

Asher, whose name meant "happy," was Jacob's ninth son. He waited to hear what his dying father's blessing for him would be. Would it be wealth? Ruling nations? Good health? Finally, it was his turn.

"Asher, my son. Your land will grow lots of good food. It will be food good enough to feed kings!"

Back in Bible times, most people were farmers. It was important for them to have good land to grow food to feed their families. But to have land good enough to grow delicious food for important kings? Well, that was a very special blessing that made Asher as happy as his name! He probably started learning to farm by planting a few seeds and watching them grow. His parents might have had to remind him to water his seeds and take care of them. He may have found that he really liked cooking and eating the food he grew.

You can be like Asher and grow food, too. Try planting a bean in a cup with some dirt. Set it in a sunny place by a window and water it a little when the soil gets dry. Maybe you'll enjoy growing things like Asher did.

Lord, help my seeds to grow.
But more important than that,
help me to grow into a person
who lives for You. Teach me
to be my best for You.

The Great Outdoors

Naphtali is a deer running free that
gives birth to lovely fawns.

Genesis 49:21 MSG

Are you ever compared to an animal? Maybe your parents have said you're a monkey because you like to climb on things. Or a honey bunny because you give good hugs. Or maybe on a grouchy morning they even called you a growly bear!

Naphtali's dad, Jacob, blessed him by saying he was a deer running free that gives birth to lovely fawns. He had watched his son grow from a boy to a man. He knew he loved to be outdoors and run in the fresh air. He loved the freedom the big outdoors offered.

Just as Naphtali wasn't *really* a deer, he didn't *really* give birth to lovely fawns either. Jacob probably meant that his son was creative and made many beautiful things. Or maybe he was someone who tenderly cared for others as a mother would care for her children. Either way, it's clear that Jacob loved his son and was proud of him.

Do you like to play outside? Do you run fast and enjoy the wind blowing in your hair? Do you make beautiful things or lovingly care for others? Then you're like Naphtali! But however God made you, He loves you very much!

Thank You, God, for the awesome
world You made for us to enjoy.
Help me to take good care of it
and the people around me.

Strong for Him

Thank You, God, for giving me strength.

"He gets his power from the Mighty God of Jacob."

Genesis 49:24 ICB

Joseph was the little brother to ten older brothers. But his father, Jacob, liked Joseph the most. It wasn't right, but the Bible says that's the way it was. Because Jacob loved Joseph best, he gave him a special blessing.

He said Joseph was strong even when people weren't nice to him. But most important, Jacob told Joseph, "Your power comes from the Mighty God of Jacob. And your strength comes from the Shepherd, the Rock of Israel" (Genesis 49:25 ICB).

We know God's the only One who can give us real strength and power and so did Joseph. We're like an electrical cord that is plugged into our power outlet—God.

Joseph may have felt that he wasn't very strong or brave compared to his big brothers. Sometimes we feel we can't do anything right. Or that we aren't big enough to do important things. But when we pray and read the Bible, we plug into the greatest power source—God. And, like Joseph, we can do amazing things.

Believe in God. He'll make you strong and powerful. You won't feel so small anymore—you'll feel like a giant!

Help me to trust You, God.
There are lots of things I can't
do yet, but I know You'll help
me to be strong for You.

Invisible Teacher

"All your children will be taught by the Lord. And they will have much peace."

Isaiah 54:13 ICB

Do you have a favorite teacher? It could be a teacher at school, your Sunday school teacher, or even your mom or dad. The Bible talks about a teacher we all have but have never seen. Can you guess who it is?

It's God! The Bible book of Isaiah says, "All your children will be taught by the Lord. And they will have much peace." Everyone starts out as a child. So we are all taught by God.

How can we learn from an invisible teacher? God teaches us through the Bible. It's His instruction manual for how we should live. When we listen to His Word and do what it teaches, we'll have a happier life. That doesn't mean nothing bad will ever happen to us. But if something bad does happen, God will help us get through it. We won't have to be so afraid. That's what His peace does for those who trust Him.

So don't forget to be a good listener to the teachers you can see and especially to the One you can't!

Dear God, I want to be a good student who learns from You. Help me to do what Your Word says.

A Parent's Joy

Children are a gift from the Lord. They
are a reward from him. . . . Blessed are
those who have many children.

Psalm 127:3, 5 NIrV

The day you were born was one of the happiest days of your parents' lives. They probably have pictures of you when you were a baby. You may have been crying in some of them. Or maybe your parents were feeding you, giving you a bath, or just holding you so you'd feel loved. They did important things to help you grow up healthy and happy.

But did you know you do important things for your parents, too? You give them great joy just by being their child. They love to hear you laugh. It makes them proud when you learn something new. And most of all, when you follow God by obeying your parents and being kind, they can almost burst with happiness!

The Bible says children are a gift

from God. You may not fit in a box with wrapping paper and a bow on top, but you're probably the best present your parents ever got. Give them an extra-special hug tonight and tell them how much you love them. Then watch the joy spread across their faces.

Dear God, thank You for
my parents. I love them.
Help me to make them happy
just by being myself.

Always Obey

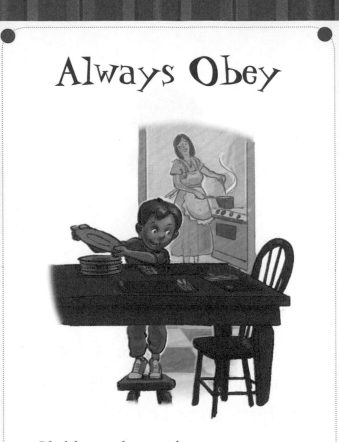

Children, always obey your parents,
for this pleases the Lord.

Colossians 3:20 NLT

Has your mom or dad ever asked you not to do something, but you went ahead and did it anyway? Maybe you even pretended you didn't hear what your mom or dad said. How did you feel about that? Did it end up the way you wanted it to?

Usually, if you disobey a parent, you'll get in trouble. It's not a very happy ending for you or that parent. Why not obey even when you don't feel like it? You may feel a little angry at first, but later you'll notice a spark of happiness deep down inside. You'll know you did the right thing.

Our Bible verse says children must *always* obey their parents because this pleases the Lord. Doing what your parents say every time is hard. You may think your parents are mean or that you have a better way to do things. Sometimes you just aren't in the mood to do what they ask. But when you obey the first time they ask you to do something, it not only makes them happy, it makes *you* feel great! Most important, it pleases God. So get up and obey quickly. You'll be glad you did.

Lord, I don't think I can obey
my parents every time. I need
Your help to do it. Will You
please help me? Thank You.

Remember

Remember to always tell the truth.

My son, keep your father's commands. Don't forget your mother's teaching. Remember their words forever. Let it be as if they were tied around your neck. They will guide you when you walk. They will guard you while you sleep. They will speak to you when you are awake.

Proverbs 6:20–22 ICB

How is your memory? Do you remember songs from TV commercials? Do you find it easy to retell jokes you've heard? How about the things your parents teach you about what's right and what's wrong? Do you remember them?

In our Bibles, Solomon was the wisest man ever. He knew that parents always want the very best for their children. That's why they teach you right from wrong. They don't want you to get into trouble or hurt yourself. They want you to follow God's ways because they know it will bring you the best life possible.

Have you ever worn a scarf around your neck in the winter? Were you warmer and more comfortable? Solomon said you should wear your parents' teaching around your neck like a scarf. You'll be more comfortable when you let their lessons wrap around you. You'll feel warm inside as you listen to their voices reminding you to make good choices. When you remember what they said, doing the right thing will become easier to do.

Work on remembering what your parents say. Follow their rules even when they're not around. You'll feel as snug and warm as when you wear your favorite scarf.

God, thank You for my parents.
Sometimes I forget what they
teach me. Help me to listen care-
fully to them so I can live
my best for You.

Wise Guy

A wise child brings joy to a father.
Proverbs 10:1 NLT

What makes your parents really happy? Playing golf? Watching a movie? Reading a book? The Bible tells us what brings your mom and dad the greatest joy. It's you!

When you make good choices and live the way God tells you to in His Word, it makes your parents' day. Think about it. What happens when you make bad choices? You get in trouble or you might even find yourself in a dangerous situation, right? Your parents want you to be happy and safe. It's no fun when you get punished. And your parents don't like to punish you when you disobey either. But they know they have to so you'll grow into the boy or girl God wants you to be.

If you obey and choose to do the right thing, your parents won't have to be sad about correcting you. They'll be happy because you made a wise choice and so will you!

So be a wise guy. Make your dad and mom's day by obeying the first time. Good choices make everyone glad!

God, I want to be wise and make
my parents glad. But most of
all I want to make You happy.
Help me to listen and obey.

Promise Keeper

So know that the Lord your God is God. He is the faithful God. He will keep his agreement of love for a thousand lifetimes. He does this for people who love him and obey his commands.

Deuteronomy 7:9 ICB

Has someone ever broken a promise to you? I hope not, but if they did, how did it make you feel?

There is Someone you can always count on to keep His promises to you. God has never, ever broken a promise to anyone. And He never will. Our Bible verse in Deuteronomy says that He is the faithful God. That means you can depend on what He says. If He says it, then it will happen. He'll keep His promise of love for "a thousand lifetimes"! Who does He do that for? Everyone who loves Him and obeys His commands.

I know you love God. And I bet you try to obey what the Bible teaches, too. Sometimes you may not do it exactly right, but God understands that everyone makes mistakes. He loves you anyway and still keeps His promises to you. Keep loving God and trying to do what He says in His Word, and He will be proud of you.

God is the greatest promise keeper in the world. You can count on Him to be there for you every time.

Lord, I'm glad I can be sure
You'll keep Your promises. Help
me to love You more and more
and follow Your commands.

Blessings or Curses

Today I'm letting you
choose a blessing or a curse.
Deuteronomy 11:26 ICB

Moses had a big job to do. God asked him to lead His chosen people, called Israelites, out of Egypt, where they had been slaves and were treated mean. Three million people! Moses didn't think he could do it. But God said, "I'll help you."

So Moses said yes.

As the people wandered in the desert, God gave Moses the Ten Commandments. These were rules to teach them how God wanted them to live. Moses told the Israelites God's rules. Then he said, "Today I'm letting you choose a blessing or a curse. You will be blessed if you obey God's rules. But you will be cursed if you don't obey them." A blessing means good things will happen to you. A curse means bad things will happen.

God gives us the same choice today. We can choose to obey Him and do our best to live the way He wants us to, or we can choose to do things our own way. Depending on the choice we make, we will be blessed by God or cursed by Him. God loves to bless us, and it makes Him sad when we decide not to follow Him. Which will you choose?

Dear God, I want to make good
choices, but I don't always know
what's right. Help me to follow
You and obey Your Word,
the Bible.

Superhero

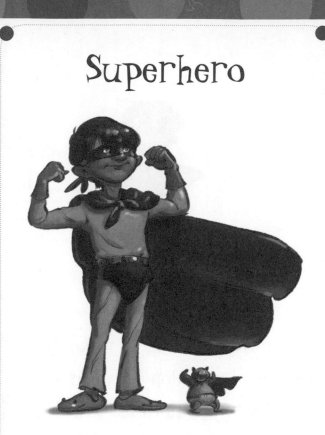

"God isn't a mere man. He can't lie.
He isn't a human being.
He doesn't change his mind."

Numbers 23:19 NIrV

Who's your favorite superhero? What special powers does he or she have? There's a superhero that's stronger, more powerful, and more awesome than any other. God is the best superhero of all. Our Bible verse in Numbers 23:19 says God isn't a human like us. Here's the best part—He can't lie. And He doesn't change His mind.

Humans may seem strong sometimes. But all humans can get sick or hurt and even die. And no matter how good a human is, everyone sins and lies at some time. But not God. He never gets sick or hurt. And He'll never die, because He's immortal. That means He *can't* die. God never sins or lies or does anything wrong. We can trust Him completely.

When He says something, it will happen. He doesn't change His mind. God says in John 3:16 that He loved the world so much that He gave us His one and only Son. That means He always loves us, no matter what we do or how good or bad we are. He won't change His mind.

Now that's a superhero who's worth worshipping!

Thanks for being a superhero
that I can always trust, God.
I'm glad You don't lie or change
Your mind. I love You.

Forever and Ever

Lord, your word is everlasting.
It continues forever in heaven.
Psalm 119:89 ICB

Everlasting is a long time. It's forever! You know how it seems to take a really long time for Christmas or your birthday to come each year? Everlasting is a lot more than a million times longer than that. But when you're talking about something *good* lasting that long instead of having to wait for something, it's wonderful!

God's Word, the Bible, is everlasting. Unlike your favorite shirt or pajamas, you'll never outgrow the things it teaches. The Bible is true and it can always help you no matter how young you are now or how old you'll be later. Our verse says God's Word "continues forever in heaven." That means it's not going anywhere, and it isn't going to change just because we do. What it says is true, both now and when you grow up.

That's a good, solid foundation to build your life on! Read your Bible and do what it says. You can count on God's Word to lead you in the right direction forever, no matter what happens to you. It's trustworthy and true, just like God.

God, sometimes I don't feel like
reading Your Word. Help me
to want to read my Bible and
spend time with You.

Yes-Man

Thank You, Jesus, for dying on the cross for my sins.

God has made a great many promises. They are all "Yes" because of what Christ has done.

2 Corinthians 1:20 NIrV

Have you ever heard of a "yes-man"? It's someone who does whatever someone tells him to do. He agrees with whatever that person says. That can be dangerous because the person he agrees with may ask him to do something he shouldn't.

But we can always say yes to God. He is always right. He'll never ask us to do something wrong. Jesus was God's best yes-man. He never sinned, because He always did what His Father asked. Our Bible verse says God made many promises. Jesus stamped His "yes" on each promise because He believed whatever God said would happen. God asked Jesus to do many of the same things He asks us to do. He wanted Jesus to obey

His parents, be kind to others, and be friends with Him. But then God asked Jesus to do something He will *never* ask us to do. He asked Jesus to die for our sins. Jesus trusted God so much He even said "yes" to that!

We can trust God, too. He loves us just as much as He loves Jesus. Will you be a yes-man for God?

God, it's hard to trust Someone
I can't see. Help me to say "yes"
to whatever You ask me to do.

Sweet Dreams

"Let the one the Lord loves rest
safely in him. The Lord guards him
all day long. The one the Lord
loves rests in his arms."

Deuteronomy 33:12 NIrV

Do you have trouble sleeping? Sometimes it's hard to close your eyes and slow down after a busy day. Worries may haunt you when you go to bed. Fears like to creep in when it's dark.

Some people count sheep when they can't get to sleep, but I have a better idea. The next time you have trouble falling asleep, think of Jesus, the Good Shepherd, and remember today's Bible verse. *You're* the one the Lord loves, and you can rest safely in Him. He's guarding you all day and all night. Picture yourself sitting in God's lap, snuggling close. His strong arms wrap around you, and your head rests on His chest as He rocks you. Can you hear His big God-heart beating? God is crazy about you! He has promised you His love and protection. He'll give you a safe rest all night long. No need to be afraid.

Psalm 121:3 says, "The LORD is your protector, and he won't go to sleep or let you stumble" (CEV). God stays awake all night to watch over you.

So close your eyes and enjoy a peaceful sleep. God is close. He won't leave your side. Sweet dreams!

Thank You, God, for being with
me while I sleep. Calm my fears
and help me to trust in You.
Good night.

Life Plan

Lord, you will do everything
you have planned for me.

Psalm 138:8 NIrV

God has a life plan for you. I wonder what it is! Maybe you'll be a scientist who discovers new planets, or a stay-at-home mom. Perhaps you'll be a missionary across the ocean or a good neighbor in your own town.

You don't have to know God's plan for you right now. You just have to keep loving Him and doing what His Word says. As you grow older and become interested in new things, you may get a clue about God's plan for you. Or you may discover things you *don't* like to do! That's okay because God made you just right so you can do the things He wants you to do as you grow up. The things you don't like to do probably aren't what God has in mind for you. But pay close attention to what you *do* like. Do you enjoy drawing? Reading? Music? Building things? Spending time with younger children? Helping older people? Maybe God will help you use those things to serve Him as you grow up.

God is shaping you into the person He wants you to be, so you can do His life plan just right!

God, I'm glad You have a plan
for me. Thank You for showing
me Your plan little by little as
I grow up. I love You.

Kingdom Kid

"So don't be afraid, little flock. For it gives your Father great happiness to give you the Kingdom."
Luke 12:32 NLT

Some days it seems as if nothing goes right. You get in trouble for things that you didn't mean to do. It might even seem as if God is trying to trick you and make you mess up. Guess what? God is on your side. He wants to help you do the right thing. He wants you to be in His kingdom, and He can't wait to spend forever with you.

Our verse says it makes God really happy to give His kingdom to you. He looks forward to the day when He'll send Jesus back to the earth to set up this kingdom. It's going to be a huge party, and you'll be one of His kingdom kids! You'll be a prince or princess! We'll enjoy a wonderful meal together with believers from all over the world. We'll even get to see people who loved Jesus but died before He returned. They'll be alive again, and it will be a wonderful celebration.

Most of all, we'll get to live with God. Just like us, He looks forward to that great day when we can live together forever. What a happy day that will be!

God, I'm glad You want to be with me forever. That's what I want, too. I have a big hug to give You when I see You in Your kingdom.

Tender and Kind

Dear God, it's been a bad day. Thanks for always being here to listen to me.

A father is tender and kind to his children. In the same way, the Lord is tender and kind to those who have respect for him.

Psalm 103:13 NIrv

Think about a time you had a bad day and felt sad. Maybe you went to your mom or dad to talk about it. What did you hope your mom or dad would do? Maybe hug you close and let you cry. Or whisper, "I love you and everything will be all right." You probably wanted someone to be kind and tender to you.

Your mom and dad sometimes have a bad day, too. They may be too tired to listen as much as you'd like. Maybe they're busy doing things like making supper or mowing the lawn. But even if it seems they don't have enough time for you, they always wish they did. They love you very much.

Whether your parents do what you

hope for on those days or not, you can always count on God to listen to you. He's never in a hurry or too busy to hear what's bothering you. God is always kind to anyone who respects Him. And He can always help you with your problems.

So talk to your parents whenever you can. But don't forget to talk to God, too. He's always there for you.

Thank You, God, for being so
kind and gentle to me. I know
You care and will always listen
when I talk to You.

Do Right

Blessed are those who always do
what is fair. Blessed are those
who keep doing what is right.

Psalm 106:3 NIrV

It's important to be fair to others. Nobody likes someone who cheats or is dishonest. That makes God sad.

Sometimes your friends might do something you know isn't right or fair. What should you do? It takes a lot of courage to tell them what they did wasn't right. You might suggest another way of doing things. You shouldn't go along with your friends if you know they're doing something wrong.

Our verse says blessed, or happy, are those who "do what is fair" and "keep doing what is right." You may have to choose to do what is right over and over again. You should do the right thing as many times as you have the chance.

Even grown-ups have to choose to do the right thing again and again. Galatians 6:9 says, "We must not become tired of doing good. We will receive our harvest of eternal life at the right time. We must not give up!" (ICB).

So keep practicing doing what's right while you're young so you'll be really good at it by the time you're all grown up. Eternal life is worth working for. Don't give up!

God, I want to live a happy life by being fair and doing what is right. Help me not to get tired of doing good.

Curses!

The Lord your God would not
listen to Balaam. He turned the
curse into a blessing for you.
The Lord your God loves you.

Deuteronomy 23:5 ICB

Balaam was a prophet. A king named Barak said he would pay Balaam a lot of money to say bad things about God's special people, the Israelites. Balaam tried to do it, but he just couldn't. He had to say what God told him to say and nothing else. But this was a big problem because he knew it would make King Barak mad.

So three times Balaam went off to talk to God. Each time God told Balaam not to say bad things about the Israelites, but to bless them instead. When Balaam told King Barak that God would bless Israel, the king frowned. "I told you to curse the Israelites, but you keep blessing them!"

Balaam answered, "I can only say

what God tells me to say. I cannot dis-obey God."

Balaam did the right thing to obey God, even though it was hard. Have you ever had to do that? Was it easy or hard? Pray for God to help you be strong enough to do what's right even if you're the only one doing it, like Balaam.

Dear God, I want to do the right thing. Help me to be strong for You and make good choices even when it's hard.

The Best Reward

"So love your enemies. Do good to them,
and lend to them without hoping to get
anything back. If you do these things,
you will have a great reward."

Luke 6:35 ICB

Have you ever seen a poster offering a reward for a lost dog? If the reward is ten dollars, you might keep your eyes open for the puppy. But if it were a thousand dollars, you might spend *lots* of extra time trying to find it! The amount of the reward tells you how important something is to the person offering it. The bigger the reward, the more important your help is to that person.

The Bible tells how we can earn a huge reward. All we have to do is love our enemies and do good to them. If we lend them something, we shouldn't worry if they don't give it back. If we do these things, we'll have a great reward. Who do you think put up that reward poster? God posted it in our Bibles in Luke 6:35. And since He offers such a huge reward, we know it's important to Him that we do it.

Is it easy to love your enemies? No. Finding a lost dog isn't easy either. But doing what God asks is always worth the reward He offers—living forever with Him! That's better than a million dollars!

God, it's hard to love people
I don't like. Help me to love
them anyway and to look
for something good in them.
I want Your reward.

The Big "If"

God, help me
to forgive.

"If you forgive others for the things
they do wrong, then your Father in
heaven will also forgive you for the
things you do wrong."

Matthew 6:14 ICB

Has someone ever made you really mad? You knew you should forgive that person, but you just didn't want to! You wanted to stay mad! Why should you forgive, after the mean thing he did?

Forgiving people is the right thing to do, and it makes God happy. But there are two other reasons you should forgive.

The first reason is in our verse. It says *if* you forgive others, then God will forgive you, too. "If" means it's a choice. You don't have to do it. But if you do, then God will forgive you for your sins. That means if you don't forgive, God won't either. That's probably part of the reason it makes God sad when we don't forgive. He loves to forgive us.

The second reason is that forgiving makes *us* feel better. It doesn't make the wrong thing that person did okay. But when we stay mad, it makes our tummies hurt and we become not-so-nice people. Then we might go around making others mad, too, just as the person who hurt you did!

So forgive others, then God can forgive you. We all make mistakes and need forgiveness.

Dear God, help me to not
stay mad at people, but help
me forgive them. Thank You
for forgiving me when I
forgive others.

Truth Telling

But God is faithful and fair. If we
admit that we have sinned, he will
forgive us our sins. He will forgive
every wrong thing we have done.
He will make us pure.

1 John 1:9 NIrV

Have you ever broken something that your parents said not to touch? Did you tell them what happened right away, or did you wait until they found the broken pieces?

It's scary to admit when you've done something wrong. You might get in trouble. Your parents might get mad. Even if you don't tell, there's that icky feeling inside, knowing you're keeping a bad secret.

I've got good news for you! God never gets mad when you come to Him and tell Him you did something wrong. He may feel sad that you made a bad choice, but He's always glad you told Him. He wants to forgive you and help you try to do better next time. Some unhappy things may still happen because you sinned, but that's only God helping you learn not to do it again. He's always fair, no matter what. He wants to help you be clean and pure inside.

And guess what? Your parents feel the same way. They'd rather have you tell them when you do something wrong than find out later on their own. So take a deep breath, and tell them the truth. God will help you.

Lord, I want to be pure.
Help me to be brave enough
to tell my parents the truth
when I do something wrong.
Thank You for loving me.

Mind Reader

"I will provide for their needs before they ask. I will help them while they are still asking for help."

Isaiah 65:24 ICB

Have you ever hurt yourself and run crying to your parents? Mom or Dad may have had a hard time understanding what was wrong because you couldn't stop crying long enough to speak. Unless you were bleeding, no one could tell why you were so upset. Maybe you were asked to show where it hurt.

Your parents love you and hate to see you hurting or sad. God is the same way. He wants to make you feel better, just like your mom and dad. But there's something different about God. He knows what's wrong even *before* you come crying to Him. And by the time you settle down enough to tell Him, He's already getting you the help you need. That's because God sees everything that happens to you and knows how you feel about it. He's always with you and can read your mind!

So the next time you run to your mom or dad in tears, remember that God is already busy working on the answer to your problem. He'll help you before you even have time to ask, because He loves you very much.

God, thanks for always being
with me and knowing just what
I need. I trust You to take care
of everything when I get hurt.

Getting Even

"May the Lord bless you for what you have done. You have shown a lot of good sense. . . . You have kept me from using my own hands to get even."

1 Samuel 25:33 NIrV

King David and his men had been traveling a long time. On this trip, they had to pass through land belonging to a man named Nabal. They hoped he would be kind to them and give them some food and water. After all, David had been kind to Nabal as he traveled through his land.

But Nabal was mean and wouldn't help David and his men. One of this mean man's messengers ran to Nabal's wife, Abigail, and told her, "Nabal refused to help King David!" The messenger was afraid David would kill his master. Abigail quickly took lots of food and drinks to the king and told him how sorry she was for the way her husband acted. She told David, "Don't do anything wrong as long as you live" (1 Samuel 25:28 NIrV). She encouraged him to do what would please God.

David thanked her for keeping him from trying to get even with Nabal. He knew God would deal with Nabal's bad behavior.

Do people sometimes make you mad? Do you want to get even with them or hurt them back? God wants us to be kind and loving. Leave the getting even to Him.

God, sometimes I get so angry
that I want to hurt people. Help
me to be kind and to leave the
getting even to You.

Food for Thought

He provides food for those
who have respect for him. He
remembers his covenant forever.

Psalm 111:5 NIrV

Have you ever heard your parents worrying about how they'll be able to pay their bills? Or maybe you asked for something at the store and they said, "No, we don't have enough money."

There are a lot of things we want—but only a few things that we really *need*. We need food and water. We need a place to live. We need clothes. Most of all, we need Jesus to take our sins away.

Our verse today promises that God will give food to those who respect Him. It doesn't say the food will be your favorite meal, complete with ice cream for dessert. But He always gives us just enough food for each day. It might be vegetables. It could be steak! Or it might be pizza or a peanut butter and jelly sandwich.

Our verse says God remembers His covenant forever. A covenant is a promise. He'll always remember to give you food if you remember to respect Him. Respect is to look up to someone or to honor them. One way you can do that is by thanking Him for whatever food He gives you today—whether you like it or not!

Thank You, God, for all the
different kinds of food You
give us. I wish they all tasted
as good as_____.
But even if they don't, thank
You anyway!

No Worries

"So don't worry. Don't say, 'What will we eat?' Or, 'What will we drink?' Or, 'What will we wear?' People who are ungodly run after all of those things. Your Father who is in heaven knows that you need them."

Matthew 6:31–32 NIrV

What things worry you? Maybe being left with a new babysitter? Or a hard test at school? Or listening to your parents argue? There are plenty of things that cause us to worry. So what can you do when worry takes over?

When you feel that yucky worry feeling sneaking up on you, the best thing you can do is pray. If something bothers you, then it matters to God, too. He cares about whatever makes His children feel bad. But He's not at all surprised by our worries! Our verse says that God knows exactly what we need and what worries us, and He will take good care of us. So we don't need to worry like people who don't know God. They don't understand how powerful God is and how much He can help them. But we know we can trust God to fill all our needs. No worries!

So next time worry creeps into your mind, remember to turn to God. Ask Him to help you not be afraid. He loves to take care of you, and you can trust Him to make your worries disappear. What a relief!

God, I know I can trust You, but sometimes I still worry. Help me to talk to You about my worries and help me not to be afraid.

"I'm a Branch!"

"I am the vine. You are the branches.
If anyone remains joined to me, and I
to him, he will bear a lot of fruit. You
can't do anything without me."

John 15:5 NIrV

Have you ever grown a plant? You had to put it in sunlight and water it. What happened if one of the green, healthy stems broke off the plant? Did the stem keep growing or start to die?

Jesus said He's like a vine, and we're like branches of the vine. Just like any other plant, the branches have to stay attached to the plant or they soon die. They can't do anything without the vine! But if they stay attached to it, then they grow strong and makes fruit or flowers.

If we stay joined to our Vine, Jesus, we'll stay strong and grow into the people God means for us to be. What will our "fruit" look like when we stay connected to Jesus? Galatians 5:22–23 tells us, "But the fruit the Holy Spirit produces is love, joy and peace. It is being patient, kind and good. It is being faithful and gentle and having control of oneself. There is no law against things of that kind" (NIrv).

So stay joined to Jesus by reading your Bible, praying, and living your best for Him. Because you can't do anything without your Vine!

Jesus, I want to stay connected to You. Let's hold hands and never let go! Help me to grow good fruit that pleases You.

"Prove It!"

"When you bear a lot of fruit,
it brings glory to my Father.
It shows that you are my disciples."
John 15:8 NIrV

"You're not a Christian."

"Yes, I am!"

"Prove it!"

What would you do if someone said that to you? How could you make someone believe that you love Jesus?

In our verse today, Jesus tells us the answer. "When you bear a lot of fruit, it brings glory to my Father. It shows that you are my disciples." Disciples of Jesus love Him and follow His teaching. If we bear lots of fruit, it makes God happy and shows that we're Christians.

What kind of fruit does He mean? Apples and oranges? No. It's the fruit we learned about in Galatians 5:22–23. When we love people and are joyful and peaceful, it shows others that we are followers of Jesus. If we're patient, kind, and good when others get impatient, mad, and rude, people see that we're different from everyone else. And when we do what we say we'll do and are gentle and self-controlled, people want to be around us because Jesus shines through us.

So prove you're a friend of Jesus by bearing lots of fruit. And when you do, you'll make God's day!

Lord Jesus, thank You for telling us how to prove we're Your followers. Help me to be fruity for You!

Extraordinary

So tell my servant David, "The Lord who rules over all says, 'I took you away from the grasslands. That's where you were taking care of your father's sheep and goats. I made you ruler over my people Israel. I have been with you everywhere you have gone. . . . Now I will make you famous. Your name will be just as respected as the names of the most important people on earth.'"

2 Samuel 7:8–9 NIrV

David of the Bible was once just a kid with chores to do just like you. He was no one special. One of his chores was watching his dad's sheep. He might have wanted to play, but instead he watched the sheep.

David grew into the teenager who killed the giant Goliath. Later, he became king of Israel. God made a special promise to David that He would make him famous and that his name would be known all over the world. That sounds pretty important! God promised this because David loved God very much. God saw David trying to do the right things and obeying his parents and God as he grew up. He did his chores and tried not to complain.

God told David He had been with him everywhere he'd been—from the pastures where he cared for the sheep to the king's palace. God took an ordinary kid and helped him become an extraordinary giant slayer and king!

Maybe you feel ordinary now, but God has great plans for you, too. He will be with you wherever you go, just as He was for David. I wonder what God will do for you?

God, help me to do my chores without complaining. I want to grow up to be someone important in Your eyes, like David. Please be with me wherever I go.

Good Gifts

Children are a gift from the Lord.
They are a reward from him.

Psalm 127:3 NIrV

Do you like to get gifts? That's what makes your birthday so much fun, right? What's the best gift you ever got? Who gave it to you?

Your mom and dad got a wonderful gift a few years ago—something they wanted very much. They could hardly wait until it arrived. They planned and prepared so they'd be ready to receive this special present. They might have even counted the days until it arrived. Do you know what that special gift was? It was you! Do you know who gave them that gift? It was God. You are one of their most precious gifts ever.

God loves to give gifts to His children. That includes your parents, even though they're all grown up and don't look much like children anymore! The Bible tells us in James 1:17 that "every good and perfect gift is from God" (NIrV). So whenever you get a gift you really like, don't forget to say thank you to the person who gave it to you—and to God! He's the best gift giver.

Thank You, God, for giving me to my parents. They take good care of me and I love them. Help me to always be a wonderful gift to them.

Family Pride

Grandparents are proud of their
grandchildren, and children should
be proud of their parents.

Proverbs 17:6 CEV

What things do you or your friends like most about grandparents? How are grandparents different from parents?

You and your grandparents are alike in some ways. You might look like them, or maybe even act like them. But there's something else that's the same. Do you know what it is? It's family pride. They're so proud of you and how you're growing up. They show your picture to all their friends. They think almost everything you do is wonderful!

There's someone you can be proud of, too, and that's your parents. They work hard to take good care of you. They love to be around you, and I bet you know just how to make them laugh. Our verse says, "Grandparents are proud of their grandchildren, and children should be proud of their parents." Do your parents make you proud? Do you want your friends to meet them and see how much fun they are?

When you say your prayers, remember to thank God for your awesome parents and all they do for you. I bet your parents and grandparents are thanking God for you, too!

God, thank You for my grandparents and my parents.
Sometimes we get mad at each
other, but I'm glad we can still
love each other anyway.

"Safe!"

The Lord is good. When people
are in trouble, they can go to him
for safety. He takes good care of
those who trust in him.

Nahum 1:7 NIrV

When you play tag, sometimes there's a "base" that makes you safe. When you reach that base, no one can tag you or get you out. If someone's chasing you, and you make it to the base in time, you yell, "Safe!" so they know they can't tag you. Then they have to find someone else to chase.

Today's verse says there's a safe place to go when we're in trouble, just as there's a safe place to go in tag. When we run to God by praying to Him and telling Him what's wrong, He becomes our safe place. Our verse says the Lord is good and He takes good care of those who trust in Him. It's hard to trust in a God we can't see, but He's the only One powerful enough to help us. He can do anything! Jeremiah 32:17 says, "Oh, Lord God, you made the skies and the earth. You made them with your very great power. There is nothing too wonderful for you to do" (icb).

So when you're in trouble, run to God. He's more powerful than anything you can imagine. And He loves to be a safe place for His children.

God, I feel safe when I talk to You. Thank You for listening when I tell You my troubles and for being powerful enough to help.

Fort God

The Lord is my rock and my fort.
He is the One who saves me. My God
is my rock. I go to him for safety.

Psalm 18:2 NIrV

Have you ever built a fort? What was it made of? Snow? Blankets and chairs? What's the coolest thing about being inside a fort? Sometimes forts are given names like Fort McHenry or Fort Knox. What would you name your fort?

The Bible talks about a fort, too. But this fort is better than any we could build. Our verse today says, "The Lord is my rock and my fort. He is the One who saves me. My God is my rock. I go to him for safety."

When you hold a rock in your hand and squeeze it hard, what happens? Does it squish? No, it stays strong and doesn't change. That's how God is! And because He's so strong, He can keep us safe.

During wartime, soldiers hide inside their forts or even fight from them. Forts are their place of safety. They protect them and save them from danger. That's what God does for us, too. He protects us and gives us a safe place to hide when we're afraid. So the next time you're scared, run to Fort God. He will save you and protect you.

Thank You, God, for being
my strong, safe place.
Help me remember to run
to You when I am afraid.

Showers of Blessing

"I will send down rain at the right time.
There will be showers of blessing."
Ezekiel 34:26 NIrV

I saw a movie once where it rained gumballs. If you could make it rain something besides water, what would you choose? Gummy bears? Ice cream cones? Money? They wouldn't be as good as God's rain.

God makes a wonderful promise to us in today's verse. He promises to send rain at just the right time. And not just any kind of rain—showers of blessing! What do you think that means? Remember that a blessing is something good that happens or that someone gives you.

Wouldn't it be wonderful if God rained blessings down on us? Really, He already has. Look around you. Everything you see is a blessing from God—your toys, your family, the Bible, trees, flowers, friends, animals, the sun and moon. But sometimes blessings are things we can't see like love, joy, peace, and knowing Jesus. What blessing would you like God to rain down on you and your family?

Our verse says He'll send *showers* of blessing. Not just a little drizzle or sprinkle, but a downpour! God loves to bless His people. So put up your umbrella and get ready for rain!

I like to run in the rain, God.
Help me to enjoy Your
showers of blessing as much
as I love getting wet. Thank
You for blessing me.

Good from Bad

We know that in everything God
works for the good of those who love
him. They are the people God called,
because that was his plan.

Romans 8:28 ICB

Sometimes really bad things happen to people, even very nice people who love God. It's hard to understand. There aren't any answers to why those things happen. They just do. Parents lose jobs, people get sick and die, bad storms come, and some moms and dads get divorced. Those are scary times in our lives.

But there's always hope, if you love God. He can do anything! He can even make good things come from bad situations. Our verse today promises that in *everything* "God works for the good of those who love him." Everything! Even if it's a bad thing, God can turn it around and make something good come from it. Things may not end up as they were before, but there will be a new kind of good for you, perhaps even better than it was before. Maybe you'll learn something that will help you in your life, or maybe you'll become better friends with God because of it.

So when things are going rough and bad things happen, remember you can trust God to work things out for your good. Because you love Him and He loves you.

God, when things change,
sometimes I get scared. I want
things to stay the same. Help me
to trust You to bring good out
of what seems bad.

Big Brother

"Anyone who does what my
Father in heaven wants is my
brother or sister or mother."

Matthew 12:50 NIrV

How many people are in your family?

Did you know you have a brother that you might not have counted?

Once, when Jesus was talking to some people, He told them that anyone who obeys God is part of His family. Do you obey God? Then you're Jesus' brother or sister! It's fun to be part of God's family. God is our Father in heaven and Jesus is His Son. Since we're God's children, too, that makes Jesus our Big Brother.

Some big brothers are pests. Jesus isn't that kind of brother. He's the kind who sticks up for you when other kids tease you. He'll listen to you if something's bothering you. He laughs and plays with you. He does all these things, only you can't see Him! But He's not make-believe at all. He's real!

Jesus loves children. He especially loves those who do what His Father says in His Word. Someday He'll come back for you so you can live forever with Him in His house. So keep obeying God and enjoy having such an awesome Big Brother.

Jesus, thank You for being
the best Big Brother ever.
Help me to obey God so I can
be ready to live with You
when You come back for me.

Love You Forever

But the Lord's love for those who
fear him continues forever and ever.
And his goodness continues to
their grandchildren.

Psalm 103:17 ICB

How long is forever? It's so long that it's hard to explain! It never ends. It goes on and on and on. . .more times than we can say "and on." What do you wish would last forever?

There *is* something that goes on forever. It's God's love for you. Think about that for a minute. God loves you when you praise Him. He loves you when you're at school or day care. He loves you when you're at home or at Grandma's house. God loves you when you're sad and when you're sick. He loves you when you're silly. He loves you when you're kind. He loves you when you're mad, when you're young, and when you're old. God even loves you when you disobey.

Is there ever a place or time God doesn't love you? No! Even after you die, God's love will live on in your children and grandchildren. God's love is humongous! You can be thankful that He loves you no matter what. He could never love you any more or less than He already does. Doesn't that make you want to love God right back? Well, go ahead! Blow Him a kiss!

God, I'm glad You love me
forever, on good days or bad.
I'll love You forever, too.
Help me to show You how much.

Clear Path

With all your heart you must trust the
LORD and not your own judgment.
Always let him lead you, and he will
clear the road for you to follow.
Proverbs 3:5–6 CEV

Have you ever tried to do something your own way but it ended up a big mess? Maybe your parents even told you to do it differently, but you wouldn't listen. It's hard to give up our own way and do things someone else's way. But when God says in His Word you should do something a certain way, you should listen and obey.

God always wants what's best for us. He wants to help us win. And God never makes mistakes. That's why we can trust whatever He says.

Have you ever gone hiking and the trail got kind of rocky and hard to walk on? Our verse today tells us that if we let God lead us, He'll clear the rocks off the trail so it's easier to follow Him. He wants our path to be smooth so we don't trip and get hurt.

Sometimes we don't follow God. We take a different path. But this way is always harder to walk because God only smoothes out *His* path for us. So save yourself a lot of stubbed toes and skinned knees and stay on God's trail. You can trust Him to lead you.

I hate stubbing my toe, God, so
thanks for clearing the rocks off
my path. Help me to trust You
and stay on Your path.

Mountain Climbing

Who may climb the mountain of the
Lord? Who may stand in his holy place?
Only those whose hands and hearts
are pure, who do not worship idols
and never tell lies.

Psalm 24:3–4 NLT

What does climbing the mountain of the Lord mean? It means becoming friends with God. It's worshipping and respecting Him. We're told three things to check to see if our friendship with God is growing.

The first one is having pure hands and hearts. That means you do the right things for the right reasons. Cleaning your room just to make your brother look bad is doing the right thing, but for the wrong reason. It's not having a pure heart.

The next item on the list says you shouldn't worship idols. An idol is anything you make more important than God. If you spend more time watching TV than doing what your mom or dad asks you to do, TV might be an idol for you. Or if you'd rather sleep over at your friend's than go to church in the morning, friends might become an idol for you. Nothing should be more important than God.

The last thing is never telling lies. The things we say must be completely true.

If you're getting better in these areas, then you're climbing the mountain of the Lord! So get on your hiking shoes! You're on the right trail.

God, help me to get better at all
these things. I want to become
better friends with You and
climb Your mountain.

Awesome God

Thank You, Jesus!

Lord, you are my God. I honor you
and praise you. You have done amazing
things. You have always done what you
said you would. You have done what
you planned long ago.

Isaiah 25:1 ICB

What are some of the things you like most about God? When you tell God or other people those things, you're honoring Him and praising Him just as our verse says. Living in a way that makes God happy is another way to honor and praise Him.

Isn't it neat we can say that God is ours? We can say, "Lord, You are my God," just as Isaiah did. God has enough love for all of us to share and still have plenty to go around. He's ours, and we're His.

Our verse says God has done amazing things. Can you think of something amazing God has done?

God had a plan even before He made the world, and that plan included you!

He knew people would make mistakes and sin, so He planned right from the beginning that He would send Jesus to die for our sins. He did that so we could live together with Him forever. That means you, too! God always does what He says He will do. He did what He planned long ago, and He still keeps His promises today.

What an awesome God!

Thank You, God, for always
keeping Your promises.
Help me to honor and praise
You in all that I do.

Never Alone

Those who know the Lord trust him.
He will not leave those
who come to him.

Psalm 9:10 ICB

When are you most afraid or lonely? Maybe it's when you go to a new place or at night when you're in bed. Most people, even grown-ups, feel lonely and scared sometimes, and that's okay. It's perfectly natural to feel that way.

But here's the good news—no matter how alone or afraid you feel, Someone is always with you. This Someone loves you very much and will always take good care of you. You can trust this Someone even more than your mom or dad! Can you guess who it is? It's God!

Our verse today says, "Those who know the Lord trust him." Do you know God? If you often feel afraid, try to get to know Him better. How do you get to know your friends? By spending time with them and talking to them, right? You can do the same thing with God by reading your Bible and talking to Him through prayer.

Our verse also says that God won't leave those who come to Him. So when you need a friend, talk to God. He'll stay right by your side and never, ever leave. Now that's a friend you'll want to keep forever!

God, I want You to be my
forever friend. Help me to trust
You so I'm not afraid or lonely.
Thank You for always
staying with me.

Batteries Needed

God didn't give us a spirit that makes
us weak and fearful. He gave us a
spirit that gives us power and love.
It helps us control ourselves.
2 Timothy 1:7 NIrV

Do you have a toy that takes batteries? What happens when the batteries die? The toy goes slower, and soon it doesn't work anymore. Then you have to plug it in to recharge the battery or put new batteries in so it will work again.

Did you know people are sort of like a battery-operated toy? We need to be plugged into a power source to keep working our best, too. When our batteries start running low, our spirits get weak and afraid. Our spirits are that deepest part inside us where our joys and fears live. But when we are fully charged, we have powerful, loving spirits, and we can control ourselves better. We don't get into as much trouble!

How do we recharge our batteries? By plugging into God. We need to read our Bibles and talk to Him through prayer. We need to go to church to become best friends with Him. We always need to stay connected to God. He'll keep us charged up with His Spirit—to make us powerful, loving, and in control of ourselves.

So plug into God and keep your spirit strong!

Thanks, God, for keeping me
charged up. Help me to stay
plugged into You by reading
my Bible and going to church
so I'm not afraid and weak.

Absolutely, Positively

That should make you feel like saying,
"The Lord helps me! Why should I be
afraid of what people can do to me?"

Hebrews 13:6 CEV

What's something you

feel really sure about—something that you know is absolutely, positively true?

Here's something else you can be sure of: "The Lord helps me! Why should I be afraid of what people can do to me?" The Bible says you can feel absolutely, positively sure of that. God *will* help you.

Imagine that mean kids are bothering you. How do you feel? Scared? Like running away? Mad? Now imagine that your mighty, powerful God comes and stands behind you. He towers over you and the mean kids. He doesn't say anything but stares at the bullies. You look up at Him and He winks at you and smiles. You've got God on your side! Compared to

God, the mean kids suddenly look small. They can't do anything to you! To your surprise, they run away in fear.

We can't really see God, but He's there, and He's just as real as your best friend. He was there for David when he faced the giant Goliath, and He'll be there for you, too. Absolutely, positively!

God, thanks for being on my
side. I know I can trust You
to help me whenever I need it.
Help me not to be afraid.

"I'm Rich!"

People who do what is
right will have rich blessings.
Proverbs 10:6 ICB

You know it's best to do what's right. But why is it best? Just to keep you out of trouble? Because it makes your mom and dad happy? Those are good reasons, but there's another one you may not have thought of.

Our verse today says, "People who do what is right will have rich blessings." Remember who gives us blessings? God does! Doing what's right makes God happy, and that's even better than making your mom and dad happy. If you please God by doing the right things and making good choices, you won't just receive regular old blessings. You'll receive *rich* blessings! God's blessings are often things we can't see or touch like love, peace, joy, and hope. And you can't buy them. They're things that are too good to put a price tag on. We could never have enough money to pay for blessings like that. But you'll be rich with blessings from God!

So do what is right and receive God's rich blessings. And it's nice to stay out of trouble and keep your mom and dad happy, too!

God, help me to make good
choices. I want to please You
and stay out of trouble, too.
Thank You for giving me
rich blessings.

Hold Tight

Let us hold firmly to the hope
we claim to have. The One
who promised is faithful.

Hebrews 10:23 NIrV

Do you have a blanky or a special soft toy you sleep with? Maybe you even carry it around during the day to help you feel safe and loved. These special items are sometimes called "lovies." We love them, and it almost seems as if they love us back. They snuggle with us and make us feel good inside.

What happens when someone tries to take your lovie? Do you let them have it? No! You hold tight to it and say, "Mine!" You don't let go and you fight to keep it.

There's something else you need to hold tight just as you do your lovie. It's Jesus and the hope He gives. You can love Jesus now while you're young. And if you hold on tight, you'll still love Him when you're older. He always gives you hope because He forgives you for your sins and helps you live a good life. How do we know? Because God promised it, and our verse says He's faithful. That means He always keeps His word.

So when you snuggle with your lovie tonight, think of Jesus. Hold tight to Him and the hope of the wonderful life He gives.

Thank You, God, for always
keeping Your promises. I'm glad
You love me. Help me to hold
tight to You and never let go.

Always Faithful

Even if we are not faithful,
he will remain faithful.
He must be true to himself.

2 Timothy 2:13 NIrV

Have you ever meant to do the right thing but then didn't? Maybe you broke a promise or told a lie when you knew you shouldn't. Or watched a show you were told not to watch. How did you feel afterward?

We all do the wrong thing sometimes. Even grown-ups do. But the good news is that God loves us anyway. It doesn't matter how many times we mess up, God still wants us to climb up in His lap and snuggle. While we're there, it's good to tell Him we're sorry. He won't ever try to make us feel worse about what we did. Why? Because even when we make mistakes, God is always faithful. His love for us will never change. That's just the way He is. He can't be any different. If He could, then He wouldn't be God. He has to be true to who He is.

So the next time you mess up, remember God's waiting to hold you and show you just how much He loves you. Run to Him! He's always faithful.

I can't believe how much You love me, God, but I'm glad You do. Help me to tell You I'm sorry when I need to and to do better the next time.

Your God and Guide

This God is our God for ever and ever.
He will be our guide to the very end.

Psalm 48:14 NIrV

On the count of three, name as many cool things about God as you can think of. One, two, three!

Guess what? That really awesome, cool, amazing God you just described is *your* God forever and ever. Isn't that wonderful? He'll always be your God as long as you live. He'll never change. He'll never die. He'll never lose His power. He'll always love you. This God is *your* God forever and ever.

And He will guide you to the very end—until you get old and die! He'll never get lost and lead you to the wrong place. He's a guide who knows how to get you to His kingdom so you can enjoy living with Him forever. He doesn't need a map. He already knows the best way for you to go. And He'll lead you there if you'll just follow Him. How do you do that? By reading your Bible and doing what it says. You follow Him when you pray to Him and live the way He wants you to.

So follow your God, the Guide who never gets lost. You'll love where He takes you!

I like it that You're my very
own God. Thanks for leading me
to Your kingdom by teaching me
the best way to live. Help me
to follow You.

Jesus in Me

The mystery in a nutshell is just this:
Christ is in you, so therefore you can
look forward to sharing in God's glory.

Colossians 1:27 MSG

Have you ever been told you look or act like your mom or dad? You might have your mom's hair color or your dad's funny laugh. That's because, when you were born, a little bit of them mixed together to become you! Kind of mysterious, huh?

The Bible talks about an even bigger mystery. Not only is a little bit of your mom and dad in you, but a little bit of Jesus is, too! When you love Jesus and ask Him to be in charge of your life, He comes to live inside your heart. Pretty soon you'll start looking and acting like Him. The nicest thing someone could ever say to you is, "You remind me of Jesus!"

When Jesus is in you, you can look

forward to His coming back to rescue you from all the problems of this world. When He does, you'll become exactly like Him. That's what sharing in God's glory means. We won't sin anymore, we won't cry, we won't have bad thoughts. That day will be better than Christmas!

So keep loving Jesus and learning how He wants you to live. Pretty soon you'll be just like Him.

Thank You, God, for giving me
something better than Christmas
to look forward to. Help me to
be more like Your Son, Jesus,
every day.

The Rich Life

The blessing of the Lord brings wealth.
Trouble doesn't come with it.

Proverbs 10:22 NIrV

What does it mean to be wealthy? It means being rich. Wealth usually means a lot of money. Our verse says, "The blessing of the Lord brings wealth." Does that mean everyone who loves Jesus will have lots of money? No. They'll have something even better.

God's blessings are better than all the money in the world. They help us enjoy life in ways that money can't. Money can't buy everything. It can only buy things. But God's blessing of love helps us feel special, because we know we belong to Someone special. When things aren't going very well and we're having problems, God's blessing of peace helps us to not feel so afraid. And when we feel as if we're going to burst with happiness, God's joy bubbles up and makes us happier than we ever thought possible.

Knowing that Jesus is coming back to save us from the troubles of this world gives us hope, another one of God's amazing blessings. And God's blessings don't bring any trouble with them. Only good things.

So enjoy the rich life God's blessings bring. You'll be richer than the wealthiest man in the world.

God, I'm thankful that You
give us blessings that are
better than money. Help me
to remember to look for
Your blessings every day.

"Call Me"

Mom, I need you!

"Call to me and I will answer you. I'll tell you marvelous and wondrous things that you could never figure out on your own."
Jeremiah 33:3 MSG

Did you ever wake up from a bad dream and call for your mom or dad? Maybe you had to call two or three times before one of them heard you. When your parents came, how did you feel? Did they help you understand that your dream wasn't real and you didn't have to be afraid?

As great as a parent is when you call out, God is even better. He hears you the first time you call and comes running. He whispers in your ear things you never knew, things only God knows. He reminds you that you're safe with Him.

He'll help you understand things you can't work out without His help. Like how to handle that bully at school, or how to be polite when you're blamed for something you didn't do. God will help you figure things out when you have no idea what to do. You can trust what He tells you because He loves you and always wants what's best for you.

So go ahead and call out to God. Listen for His thundering footsteps and then His soft whisper in your ear. He's got all the right answers.

God, sometimes I forget to call
out to You when I need help.
Remind me that You're there and
want to help me. I'll trust You
and listen to You.

Under Construction

God began doing a good work in you.
And he will continue it until it is
finished when Jesus Christ comes
again. I am sure of that.

Philippians 1:6 ICB

Sometimes when workers fix a road, they put up a sign that says UNDER CONSTRUCTION. That means they're still working on the road, and it may be bumpy or dusty until it's done. We have to be patient until they're done working, and then the road will be better than ever.

You know what? God put an "Under Construction" sign on you! He started working on you when you were born. He's fixing all the things that aren't very nice about you. He's helping you be nicer by smoothing off the sharp pointed words you say that hurt people's feelings. He's carving your heart so you'll obey your parents the first time they ask you to do something. God's shaping you into the best boy or girl you can be.

When will God be done with you? Not until Jesus comes back. But you can be sure that He never gives up on you, even when you make mistakes. He just keeps patiently shaping you like a soft, giant piece of clay. So don't worry if you don't always do what you know you should. God isn't finished with you yet.

God, help me to be patient while
You work on me. I want to be
my very best for You. Thank
You for not giving up on me.

Overflowing Love

I pray that your love will overflow more
and more, and that you will keep on
growing in knowledge and understanding.
Philippians 1:9 NLT

Have you ever tried to pour your own drink? Maybe you filled your glass so full it spilled out the top. What a mess!

Today's Bible verse talks about something else spilling out and overflowing. Paul, a man who lived in Bible times, told some people he would pray that their love would overflow more and more. When that happened, they would keep on growing in knowledge and understanding. He wanted their love to spill over not just a little bit, but more and more each day. He wanted them to learn and understand the things God wanted them to do.

One of the most important things God told us to do is love each other. We can make our love overflow, too! We love each other when we help someone. We show love when we cheer people up with a smile, when we show respect to people who are in charge and don't talk back to them. Those things make God happy.

So go ahead and make a big spill— with your love, that is!

God, may my love spill over
onto everyone I meet. Help my
love show them that You're my
friend, and that You'll be
their friend, too.

Good Faith

You should try very hard to add
goodness to your faith.

2 Peter 1:5 NIrV

What is faith? Hebrews 11:1 says, "Faith is being sure of what we hope for. It is being certain of what we do not see" (NIrV). We can't see God, but we're sure He's real. We have the great hope that God the Father will send Jesus back to the earth so we can live together forever. If you believe those things, even though you can't see them and don't know when they will happen, then you have faith!

Our verse today says we should add goodness to our faith. We can do that by being kind and helpful, even when we don't feel like it. It's a funny thing, but when you do the right thing, you'll always be glad you did, even when you'd rather do something else. Adding goodness to your faith makes waiting for Jesus to come back a lot easier. Our time is spent thinking of others instead of ourselves. And that's a good feeling!

Think of a way you can help someone. Then do it! You'll be adding goodness to your faith, and that makes your faith stronger.

God, please help me to
have a great big faith with
lots of goodness mixed in.
I believe in You.

Good People, Good City

The influence of good people
makes a city great. But the wicked
can destroy it with their words.

Proverbs 11:11 ICB

What do you love about the city you live in? Does it have colorful fireworks on the Fourth of July? Does it have parades on special holidays? Do the parks have fun playgrounds?

Have you ever thought about what makes a city great? Our verse says that good people make great cities. When good people decide what goes on in a city, God blesses it. But our verse also says that bad people can destroy a city by saying bad things about it.

Every few years our governments have elections. That's when the people get to choose who they think will run their city or country the best. Your mom and dad may vote in these elections. It's very important for people who love Jesus to vote so that good people will be in charge of our government.

You're not old enough to vote yet. But you can do something that's just as important. You can pray for the leaders of your city, state, and country. Pray that they'll run things in a way that pleases God. That's what makes a city great!

Lord, please let good people be in charge of my city, state, and country. Help them remember to ask You for help when they don't know what to do.

Tell the Truth

A truthful man will
have many blessings.
Proverbs 28:20 ICB

Is telling the truth hard or easy for you? Sometimes it's easy, like when your grandpa says, "Who wants ice cream?" But telling the truth can sometimes be hard. When you've done something you shouldn't and your mom says, "Did you do that?" you may feel like running and hiding under the bed. But that won't help. Are you brave enough to tell the truth even when it's hard? Even when it might get you in trouble?

Our verse today says that if you're a truthful person, you'll have many blessings. Someone who's truthful doesn't just tell the truth sometimes. He *always* does. One of the blessings of being truthful is that people can believe you. They know that what you say is true, no matter what.

When your parents trust you, they'll let you do more of the things you want to do. Why? Because being truthful and honest shows them you're growing up. They'll know that you're learning to do the right thing even when it's hard.

So tell the truth and let God's blessings rain down on you. Being trusted and known as an honest person is a wonderful feeling.

God, I'm afraid to tell the truth sometimes. Help me to be brave enough to do the right thing. I trust You to help me handle whatever happens.

Linda Carlblom is a wife, mom of three children, and Grammy to three grand-sons and one granddaughter. She loves writing children's fiction and speaking to women and kids. She's active in her local church in Tempe, Arizona. After God, her top three loves are family, reading, and cheesecake. Visit her at www.lindacarlblom.com

Also from Barbour Publishing

Full-color kids' devotionals
that are both fun and challenging!

ISBN 978-1-59310-358-3

ISBN 978-1-60260-692-0

ISBN 978-1-60260-066-9

Paperback / 5" x 7" / 256 pages

Available wherever Christian books are sold.